Why Real Estate
& Why Now?

Why Real Estate & Why Now?

The Simple Steps to Creating Long Term Sustainable Wealth Through Real Estate Investing

Kerry Lampkin

Published by Game Changer Publishing

ISBN: 979-8-9851206-3-9

GC Game Changer
PUBLISHING

www.PublishABestSellingBook.com

DEDICATION

I want to dedicate this book to my parents, Kerry Lampkin Sr. & Diane Lampkin, My wife Krystal N. Lampkin, and my Children Kiaree, Kylia, Kiel, Khari & Kiyomi Lampkin.

SPECIAL ACKNOWLEDGMENTS

To all of my mentors and Mr. & Mrs. John Christmas, Esq.
who have helped with this book.

FREE GIFTS

DOWNLOAD YOUR FREE GIFTS

Read This First

Just to say thanks for buying and reading my book, I would like to give you a few free bonus gifts, no strings attached!

To Download Now, Visit:
www.WhyRealEstateBook.com/KLFreegifts

Why Real Estate & Why Now?

The Simple Steps to Creating Long Term, Sustainable
Wealth Through Real Estate Investing

Kerry Lampkin

GC | **Game Changer** PUBLISHING

www.PublishABestSellingBook.com

Table of Contents

Table of Contents

Introduction

Hello, my name is Kerry Lampkin, real estate investor, developer, author, and your guide to acquiring real estate and more. In this book, I will be explaining "Why Real Estate and Why Now."

I first want to thank you for purchasing this book. I believe that knowledge is wealth, and this book will give you the keys to start investing. Not only will YOU be empowered, but you will also be empowered to help others. The hardest thing is getting started. I hope this book will inspire you and encourage you to get started today.

So you may be wondering, who is Kerry Lampkin, and why should I read this book? Well, let me tell you why. Not only do I have experience, but I also have great mentors who taught me everything I need to know from the mistakes they have made. It's very important to have a mentor with years of experience in the career field you may be interested in. Depending on the individual work ethic, dedication and commitment, it will allow you to experience greater success in a shorter time frame and help you avoid the past mistakes your mentor may have made. Before I had a mentor, I made many mistakes until I figured out what I was doing wrong and what I needed to start doing to avoid these costly mistakes.

Someone once told me that I would continue to live and learn in life. I found that to be very true because there are two ways to learn in life, you're either going to choose the hard way in life or choose the easy way in life. I have learned a lot from both ways. We want to keep moving forward and not dwell on our past mistakes. All of that being said, I will help you get started today.

CHAPTER 1

Building a Legacy and Why That Is Important

Let me first start by saying why it's very important to build a legacy. God is NOT going to create MORE LAND! You have to possess the land, and when you find a way to possess it, you have to keep it and not sell it, no matter how hard times may get for you... KEEP IT!! Use the God-given power that God gave us to create wealth!

President Abraham Lincoln signed the Homestead Act on May 20, 1862. On January 1, 1863, Daniel Freeman made the first claim under the Act, which gave citizens or future citizens up to 160 acres of public land provided they lived on it, improved it, and paid a small registration fee. The Government granted more than 270 million acres of land while the law was effective. Any U.S. citizen, or intended citizen, who had never borne arms against the U.S. Government could apply and lay claim to 160 acres of surveyed Government land. For the next five years, the General Land Office looked for a good faith effort by the homesteaders. This meant that the homestead was their primary residence and improved the land. After five years, the homesteader could file for his patent (or deed of title) by submitting proof of residency and the required improvements to a local land office.

The problem with this opportunity back then was that it was more challenging for people of color to take advantage of this major opportunity to possess the land. Black folks were losing their land due to the system I will talk about in my next book. The purpose of bringing this up is because I want you to see and know my motive on why I'm big on possessing the land and helping others with knowledge to keep their land and not lose it based on ignorance. My pastor used to always tell me, "It's not what you get, Kerry, it's what you keep!" but yea, back to what I was saying about the black land loss.

"Black land loss" in the United States refers to the loss of land ownership and rights by black families and farmers residing or farming in the United States. The Emancipation Proclamation freed slaves but did not provide the right to own land. After the Civil War, some states passed laws prohibiting persons of color from owning real property.[1]

After the mid-1800s, Civil War removed the slavery issue because the Southern states had seceded from the Union. So finally, in 1862, the Homestead Act was passed and signed into law. The new law established a three-fold homestead acquisition process: apply, improve the land, and file a title deed.

After learning about the black land loss in the United States, I'm passionate about helping individuals know their rights and what governmental assistance is available to them to obtain land and keep it. In

[1] wfpc.sanford.duke.edu/media/black-land-loss

addition, I want to guide people on how to possess land to build a legacy to leave generational wealth to their children.

* * *

In January 2014, I got involved in real estate, working with my parents, Kerry Lampkin Sr. and Diane Lampkin. I helped them by coordinating the purchase of their real estate property investment. I wasn't that knowledgeable about real estate at the time, but one thing about me, I will figure it out by all means. I remember when my Dad passed by a for-sale sign staked in the front yard of a home, and he asked if I could call the number to see how much the property was selling for. After calling the seller or listing agent and gathering information from my father, I began to do my due diligence on the property to verify what the seller told me, and it checked out to be a very good deal. After my parents purchased the house, I began to help set up utilities with Bluebonnet Electric Co-op. I learned a lot going through that process and setting up water with that city/county water department. The next thing I learned was how to get an estimate to get the property remodeled. We were blessed to have close family members who had experience with construction rehabs. Shout out to my older cousin Bobby Lampkin Jr. who helped us tremendously with the rehab; I learned a lot from him and his business partner Tony. Bobby prepared what he called a "punch list" for a remodel job. On the other hand, I preferred to call it a "scope of work." This scope of work provided us with a breakdown of what needed to be done and the cost.

After the rehab work was done, I was able to list the property for rent on a free listing site called Craigslist. As soon as I posted the listing, I had numerous leads for potential tenants. Once I found a qualified tenant, I quickly searched for a lease agreement rental template on Google and revised it with the tenant information that was renting the property.

I said all of that to say this. When I started learning the real estate business, I was learning as I was going, and one of the hardest things for people is to get started. I have to applaud my parents for getting started, not with just this real estate rental property they purchased, but the business they started June 21st, 1995 called, "KERRY & DIANE LAMPKIN LAWN MOWING, INC." I was around 6 years old when my parents started this company. When I was little, they would mow the lawn in these nice neighborhoods in Houston, Texas. They worked hard to save up money to purchase their first brick home. I wanted to acknowledge my parents' accomplishments because they are a prime example of leaving a legacy. When you hear me talk about legacy and citing and paraphrasing my favorite scripture about a good man leaving a heritage for his children, my parents are examples of that! They are the ones who inspired me to be an entrepreneur.

Fast forward to 2016, the Lord led me to move to Detroit, Michigan. Well, not quite Detroit but 17 minutes outside the city of Detroit. When I got settled there, I was being mentored by my Pastor Wayne T. Jackson on both the spiritual side and business sides. As I spent more time around him and others who played a role in my success, I was able to pick up the principles and qualities they had and hear the language they would say in our conversation. The network of people you around become a part of your connections.

So back in 2016, I was seeking how to do flips and how to wholesale. I went to a young man who was very successful in real estate flips, and I asked him, "How did you do it?" He told me the game is to be sold, not to be told. And I was like, wow! What? What does that mean? Like, it pretty much means he wanted to charge me for his time. And I was like, well, I wasn't really making money at the time. So, with the little information that I gathered from him, I started searching for things on the internet, such as YouTube University. I call it that because YouTube will "school you," and you can then teach yourself how to do these things.

So as I began to learn, I went ahead and started to search for my first deal. And how I did it was, I went to Craigslist. I started searching through all the pages and pages of deals, and I found one particular ad that had a house for sale for $1,000, and I was like, this can't be real because I am from Texas, properties being $40,000-$50,000 for something like a foreclosure property. So $1,000 for a property really, really, really raised a lot of red flags. But what I did was I started doing my due diligence. And when I did my due diligence, I began to research what the guy was telling me who was trying to sell me the property. It all lined up—he wasn't lying. So I took a calculated risk of wiring him $1,000. Now keep in mind the $1,000 that I wired the guy wasn't even my money. It was someone else's money I used to acquire the property when I listed the property.

So to keep a long story short, I was able to get that $1,000 with the earnest money deposit. I had to do my due diligence because I'm not reckless with other people's money. I wanted to make sure that I was confident with the deal before even bringing someone in. So I made sure that I was confident, even though it was still a risk because this guy could have bolted with that $1,000, leaving me owing the other guy the $1,000 he sent me for earnest money deposit.

I was able to do my due diligence first, and number two, I cleaned the property up and got it all nice and neat. And then I took some nice photos to repost that property back on Craigslist for $10,000. So when I posted that property on Craigslist for $10,000, that's when I had a lot of leads, and I called all those bites. It's like you are throwing out a fishing net or a fishing line with bait on it, and you get a lot of investors biting on that bait. When I did that, I made the post on Craigslist more desirable because, at first, that post wasn't as desirable.

The previous owner posted photos of a Google Map or something he found on the internet that didn't even look like it; it looked like a scam. But then, after talking to the guy, I was listening to how he spoke and how confident he was, and how much information he knew. And keep in mind, this investor was an out-of-state investor who was stressed and wanted to get out of the market—he wanted out. So that was a great opportunity for me. This was a motivated seller. Motivated sellers are good people who want to actually try to get you to lock in and get the property for them because they want out.

So to wrap this story up, whenever I got money from the potential buyer as an earnest money deposit, I wired it to the owner who was out of state. The investor told me, "If you wire me money, I'll send you the deed through the mail overnight."

I was like, "Oh, man, you know what? No, send me the deed first and then I will send you the money."

He responded with, "No, you send me the money, and I'll send the deed." So we didn't trust each other.

WHY REAL ESTATE & WHY NOW?

Someone had to take the calculated risk, and it wasn't going to be him. So I went ahead and did it and it's one of the best decisions that I ever made. You know why? Because this guy was loyal, a trusted guy. And as soon as I wired that money to him, the $1,000, I was able to cash him out and he sent me the deed. I couldn't quitclaim[2] that property into my name or record it, because he already had put the property into my name when he sent it to me. So I just had to get it recorded. Once I got that recorded, I was then able to sell and close the deal with the potential buyer that reached out to me through Craigslist. I sold it for $10,000, but I made a profit at $9,000. I'll tell you that this changed my life, because it made me believe that this can actually happen.

One of the first things you have to do in real estate is believe; you have to see yourself actually closing those deals. You have to see yourself winning. And that raised my consciousness knowing that I could do this again. Guess what? The same guy that I trusted, with whom I took a calculated risk, this guy had 12 more properties. And from there, it was a game-changer. It changed my life where I started selling each of his properties one by one, and I made over $100,000 in less than three months.

So let's talk about mindset because I'm there. Mindset: You have to have tough skin. I'm going to say that again. ***You have to have tough skin to be in this business.*** The reason why I say that is because it's not all rainbows in this business. You're going to have some failures. You're going to be stressed. It's the nature of the business. So you have to have tough skin.

---

[2] A quitclaim deed is a document that is used to transfer ownership of real estate from one party to another. Quitclaim deeds are also sometimes called quick claim deeds because they are a fast way to accomplish real estate transfers

Many people start, and one wrong thing happens, and they get discouraged and stop doing the real estate business. So it all starts with a mindset knowing that it's going to be tough. You must put the work in because, without work, nothing's going to get done. I used to tell my little brothers when they were little, "If it is to be, put that in their mind." I said, "If it is to be, it is up to me." I had them repeat that to themselves because no one in life will give you anything. You have to go for it. You have to work for it. You have to go hard. You have to fight.

The next thing I want to talk about is what you should do and what you shouldn't do in real estate. When I was making all the mistakes without having a mentor, I had a lot of failures. I was trusting people. I wasn't doing my due diligence. So that's one of the don'ts, is that you want to make sure you don't acquire a property unless you have done your due diligence. You have to do your due diligence in this business because it is a sharky business. That's what I call it. When I refer to sharky, there are some scams out there that will take advantage of you, especially if you're green. If you're green in that area, you will get taken advantage of. So you want to make sure that you do your due, I call it, do the due.

Another thing you have to know is that you're never going to take a loss. You never lose in this business. You're either going to win, or you're going to learn. And best believe I've had a lot of learning in this business—a lot of learning. So don't allow failure to stop you. You have to keep going because failure forces you to fail your way to success. That's something I heard through many of my mentors is that phrase, **you're going to fail your way to success.** I never understood that term until now.

So I'm telling you as your mentor, as you're reading this book, that you're going to learn that I kept going. I didn't let failure stop me. I kept going, and going and going; learning and learning and learning. So just know that when things come your way, when trouble comes your way, if you fail, if you take a big loss in this real estate business, or whatever you did, just know that you learned a valuable lesson. And the way to make you understand it more is that whenever you go to school, wherever you go off to college, what do you do? You learn. And what do you have to do? You also have to pay too. You have to pay their tuition. So just see that as a lesson learned and that you will never make that mistake again.

So in this book, I want to teach you how to go from surviving to thriving. And one thing I always tell the students that are in my class or whoever I come across, I always tell them, do not be a know-it-all, be a "learner-at-all" because if you're a know-it-all, it's going to stop you from receiving good information that someone is telling you based on their experience. When you learn-it-all, you're in the receiving mode. Even if you think you know it, someone might say it in a way that allows you to work even smarter instead of harder. So yeah, don't know-it-all, learn-it-all.

Alright, here we go. Sit back, strap in, and enjoy this real estate investment journey with me.

CHAPTER 2

Escaping the 9 to 5 Rat Race

This chapter is about helping those who are still working the nine to five as a part of corporate America. I want to help you break free of that and build long-term sustainable wealth and multiple income streams through real estate. Here is some advice for all the newbies out there—set goals. Goal setting was key to my success because before I met my mentor, I had to have a plan; I had to set out a plan and some goals. Once I was able to set out the goals, I was able to have a checklist of things that needed to be done for me to get to my goal. Once I began to progress on my goals, I checked things off and knew where I was. Your conscious mind doesn't know where to go; you have to tell it where to go, and it will follow the plan; it will follow the plan if you set out the plan.

Here's my advice. If you're already invested in real estate and have a lot of experience, stay evolving. You want to evolve in this business. If you fail to evolve, you will die slowly. I'm not saying physically, I'm saying in your business. Because one thing about this new generation is that there's a lot of those into computers, into their phones and apps. So you want to make yourself visible. You want to create a social media page and advertise those properties there. And you want to stay learning because there's always something new.

For example, many old school people are more into the rent rolls, having renters or tenants pay the rent. However, we live in a time where Airbnb has become very popular. I've come to find out that you make more money having an Airbnb than having a monthly payment come in each month from one tenant because you can have multiple people who rent out that house or that building as an Airbnb and make ten times as much. So the advice I want to give to all the inexperienced investors is that you need to stay evolving.

Let's talk about the big myth. The big myth in real estate is that everybody always says it takes money to make money and that you need money to start investing in real estate. I find that not to be true. Let me tell you why. I started in real estate with $0 of my own money. It was someone else's money. You have to strategize and have a strategy! It's all about coming up with a game plan. Everything starts with a game plan. Everything always has to have a strategy. When you create that strategy, such as what I did when I spoke about in my introduction how I came up with my first $1,000 to pay for a property and made $9,000 profit, and that strategy for no money down is all in this book. I'm telling you, you can either make money from investors by receiving a finder's fee, which is finding properties for investors for a flat rate commission percentage, or you can decide to do a joint venture partnership with an investor, a friend, or family member that may have the funds to invest. Someone you know in your circle that possibly may have funds for you to partner with. One thing about that is that you have to come with your A-game.

You have to come with as much knowledge about what you want their money for. Because as an investor, you have to bring something to the table. You have to have some skin in the game, whether it's going to be sweat equity or if it's going to be you putting up some money. So if you don't have the money, you have to come up with a strategy, come up with ideas, and be creative. So, to sum it all up, there are multiple ways to structure a no-money-down deal.

One of the strategies I did for no money down in this real estate business is getting a finder's fee. Let me share with you my story on how I could make money with no money down, absolutely no money down towards it, or anything out of my pocket. I structured this deal because I found out that one of my gifts is finding deals and finding properties. I've developed an eye for distressed properties owned by motivated sellers which I can buy.

I had an out-of-state investor come to visit me, and he wanted to buy multi-units. So what I began to do was look for multi-units as I was driving around whatever city I happened to be in. The first thing you want to do is find out what their need is, their preference, what they are looking for so you're not wasting your time finding all these properties. This investor told me he was looking for a multi-unit apartment building. I asked how many units? He said he didn't care, but he wanted at least four units.

When I found this property, I tried to wholesale this deal. But it got a little complicated because the seller was also trying to wholesale the deal. So what I did was I asked the guy, what would be fair to pay me in this case? Just to give you the full honest truth of how that happened, I was doing it for free. And guess what? My mentor was like, "No, no, no, no, Kerry. You need to go back to the investor and ask him to be fair and give you compensation for your time for finding that property." This is how I discovered that you could make money helping people find properties. So this was like a light bulb that turned on in my head. So thank God for my mentor who told me, "Hey, that's not right! You need to make some money off that."

So I found an eight-unit apartment building, and I then went back to him after he closed to ask for that finder's fee. I didn't want to seem like I was greedy. I don't want to seem like this is all I want from the guy; I want to build this relationship because I'm really big on relationships. But look, at the end of the day, without me, he wouldn't have found this property. So I had to look at it from a business standpoint like he's going to make millions, and he's going to make money off this property. This property's going to be worth millions. He's going to be having some good sustainable wealth, and he's going to generate a lot of money for his children's children. So, this is how I tapped into the finder's fee, is by my mentor saying I need to be compensated, and I made $1,000 on the deal. Because it wasn't one deal, it was actually two deals that I actually found this investor, but I made money without having to spend a dime out of my pocket. So, just keep in mind there are multiple ways you can structure deals with no money down.

The second point I want to get into is how I made money without any money down by wholesaling. Now, I hate to bring this up because the person reading this may feel like, "Oh, he got me." Well, look, I'm going to be quite honest. I like to be transparent. I had another deal, a multi-unit, and I sold it to another investor out of state. I got this property from the motivated seller for $17,000. I sold that property for $55,000. Keep in mind. I didn't just sell the property. I also asked for ownership equity if I found this guy a deal. So not only did I get my initial investment back, but I also had a 50/50 partnership. Well, I can't say initial investment back because I didn't even use my money, but I profited $38,000 from this deal. I got it for $17,000 on the contract and wholesaled it for $55,000, and I profited $38,000. What a deal!

Again, I was able to sell this property for $55,000 with a joint venture with another investor, and I was able to profit $38,000 and still have 50% ownership in this building. So, when we sold the property, I was able to make even more money. So not only did I make money from its sale, but I also made money when we sold it again together. So those are creative ways you can go about things without having to spend a dime.

CHAPTER 3

Investment Vehicles and Options for Building Wealth

Always remember that if you decide to do real estate wholesaling, the strategy for real estate wholesaling is to use wholesaling to build working capital so that you can purchase real estate to rehab, rent out, and actually OWN the property! That's what you call building wealth.

You have to control the deal and funds no matter what you invest in. You know why? Because it's the right thing to do. I always tell people that they want to do "the due." What that simply means is to do their due diligence. Doing your due diligence is simply researching before spending your money on it, gaining knowledge, and feeling comfortable and confident before spending a dime. So remember, be in control of the deal by doing "the due."

There are many ways to generate additional cash, income, and wealth in today's world: real estate, crypto, gold and silver, forex, network marketing, e-commerce, and more. But my love is real estate.

As many have said throughout history, land is the basis for all freedom. I agree.

When you read this book or when you are exposed to any of the topics I mention through the media, please know that the power of possessing the land is transformational.

The information I will provide in this book is a real tool essential in your journey to economic freedom. I ask you not to keep this powerful information secret. In fact, please share and discuss this transformational information with friends and family members.

Far too long and far too many families have not been able to unlock the power of real estate to create wealth and transfer generational wealth.

My love for real estate and teaching others how to acquire real estate is one of my true passions.

I hope that this book and my teaching services evidence this fact.

CHAPTER 4

Why Real Estate?

One of the things I love about real estate is the short-term and long-term investment benefits. I'll give you a story about the short-term. So the short-term is something that I always do when I want to make quick flips, where I may see a potential property that is maybe worth $50,000 that I'm able to purchase for maybe $10,000. I know that once I do a little bit of work on it, maybe I put in $15,000, that I can make a $25,000 profit off something small and simple. So I always tell my newbies to start on things like that for the simple reason that it is not as much work.

The long-term ones may take a little work because you could start the rehab process if needed when you buy-and-hold. One thing that I love about the long-term ones is that you're able to have something tangible that is an asset, bringing money to you as an appreciating asset. Properties like that are desirable. Whenever I'm buying properties, I have different categories of investments that allow me to look at the deal and say, this is my short-term, this is my long-term. So, there are definitely benefits to both short-term and long-term real estate investing.

The next thing I want to talk about is how to boss up. So one of the ways you boss up is by investing in real estate. You become your boss. You become your own boss. I remember when I was working for someone, and I needed time off, and they couldn't give me that time off, they wouldn't accept my time off request, and I told myself, *You know what? One day, I'm not going to always be in this situation. I'm going to be my own boss.* Real estate investing has helped me become my own boss—I make my own decisions.

Let's talk about asset appreciation. So, as I said before, in the long-term, and even when you buy-and-hold these properties, these properties appreciate when you put money into them. And what I mean by that is that when you begin to develop them, you begin to rehab these properties, these properties begin to appreciate, making that property more desirable and more in demand, meaning someone will pay more for it. Let's take a closer look at the steps you should be taking before you even get into an investment.

The first step is to make sure you get a contractor who will give you a quote on how much it's going to take to fix this property up.

The next thing is to hire an appraiser. You want your appraiser to come in to let you know, okay, "Kerry, you need to do it this way." I had this happen. An appraiser told me I needed to fix the property a certain way to get maximum value out of it. He told me, "There's no need to do a finished basement to this building," or to this property because all the other ones are selling for this price without finishing the basement. The appraiser said, "The only thing you're doing is spending more money on this property, and it's taking away from your profit." So you want to make sure you know how much money to put into a property before you start putting money into it. You want to have all your facts, all your information in front of you, so you can know how much money you can make with this property.

So asset appreciation, gaining more money, is one of the reasons why I love real estate. Even if you sit on the property as a buy-and-hold, somebody else will come in and buy it later on.

What about the tax benefits? You definitely do get tax benefits. Anytime you're making any money towards any investment such as real estate, you get paid and move into a different tax bracket. To combat paying too much in taxes, you could do a 1031 exchange. A 1031 exchange allows you to transfer the funds, the profit, or whatever you had from the real estate investing into a hard asset. It's kind of like a savings account, but not really. But it's known as money sitting inside real estate, a hard asset that later will actually appreciate even more. So the money's making more sitting in the property than it would be sitting in the bank. You are putting your money into a real estate investment, like properties, any type of property, whether it's commercial or residential, it's going to appreciate.

Let's talk about that long-term stability. I've learned a lot by reading books. One of my favorite authors is Robert Kiyosaki because he talks about the Rich Dad, Poor Dad. I've learned a lot from him, but one of the most impactful things is about the difference between an asset and a liability. We all know that an asset will bring money in, and a liability is something that will take money out; it will take money out of you. Real estate is one of the ways you can have long-term stability because real estate will continue to bring money in if you do it right. If you fix it up and put tenants in there, you can get a long cash flow of income coming in every month, especially multi-units.

What's the difference between investing assets versus spending and accumulating liabilities? It is very important in this real estate business to do it the right way by having a plan with an exit strategy. You want to exit before you enter. But before I go on to talk about that, let's talk about the difference between investing assets versus accumulating liabilities.

Whenever I'm going into an investment in real estate, I want to make sure that this property will bring in cash, whether it's going to be an Airbnb or if there's going to be a rental property. But you can't know these days unless you have a strategy before you enter into the deal. So you have to know what you want and know what you want to do. The thing that I loved to do was I wanted to do flips, and I knew that I wanted to have rental properties where I was able to get that income that comes in. Now, this is where I failed in my early stages of investing. I didn't have a strategy coming in. So with me not having a strategy coming in or exit strategy coming in, I was spending money, spending money, spending money with no money coming in. I had a whole year of doing rehabs with no money coming in. I did not have an exit strategy, and I just started going. I was excited about the properties. I was excited about how cheap the properties were. I was excited about getting into real estate, but I didn't have a plan. Without a plan, you will fail in this business—you will fail. So always remember, exit before you enter.

Let's move on to recession and inflation-proof investments. One of my mentors out in Florida told me about being recession-proof. This was when I was trying to get out of the mess I was in. He began to tell me that I should invest in a multi-unit because I was dealing with many residential areas at the time. And the residential properties were good, but

I wasn't making much money until I got into investing in the buildings and multi-units, you know, the commercial type of properties.

I began to take lessons, and I learned from him, and he was right. And he would say to me, "Multi-units are recession-proof, Kerry. So you want to buy multi-units."

And I was like, "Why, why multi-units?

He told me that when there is a recession like in 2008, a lot of people lost their jobs and lost their homes. It sucked for consumers, and it sucked for some investors because the consumers had to downsize. The people who lost their jobs had to downsize and go to a lower-income home. So the investors in the low-income business were the ones gaining. Like pretty much, they were secure. They were secure because people started to downsize and go into these apartment buildings because it was what people could afford. So that was recession-proof. That's why I was preaching the importance of having an exit strategy because your exit strategy will tell you when you need to buy and when you need to sell out.

Now let me tell you the benefit of this when the crash happened. The people who had money, who had saved up or who had money to invest, the people who had the money to make the right, smart moves, actually sold out. They had an exit strategy. What happened was this thing called wealth transfer. These guys were able to buy these properties, pennies on a dollar.

To sum this all up, you want to make sure you have an exit strategy before entering into real estate investing and that multi-units are recession-proof.

CHAPTER 5

What Kind of Real Estate Investing?

In this chapter, I will share all the different ways you can play this amazing real estate investing game and why it's important to take a diversified approach. You don't want to put all your eggs in one basket. So let me tell you the different types of real estate.

1. Residential
2. Commercial
3. Commercial strip centers - such retail buildings and things like that.
4. Industrial buildings
5. Land

Let's begin with residential, which deals with anything that's up to four units. You can have a four-unit that is considered commercial, but generally, if it's four units or less, that's considered a residential property. So if I were to go back with the knowledge that I know now, I would want my first home to be a four-unit apartment building. Why? Because, as I said before, I want assets, not liabilities.

One thing about an asset, an asset brings money in, and a liability takes money out. So even as a homeowner, owning the home is really not an asset because I'm living in it, and I'm paying that mortgage every month. But if you have something like a multi-unit, and you live in one unit and have the other three units rented out, that's credited to you as income. So now that's money coming in; that becomes an asset. So there are all types of strategies you can utilize.

The home that I have in Michigan, I fixed up the whole bottom level, so it became an actual income home. The mortgage payments that I make every month can be paid for by Airbnb clients. So that's a strategy that I want to share with you guys to think about whenever you're making these investments.

Let's talk about the commercials. So five units and above is considered a commercial building where if you need to seek financing for that multi-unit, you can get it at top value. And those dealing with apartment buildings, commercial deals with strip centers, and so on, anything that is industrial, many things that have retail shops, and apartment buildings, those types of buildings, that's where you make your money.

I like to use quadrants to explain. You draw a square. You go vertical, and you go horizontal. On the left side of this quadrant, this is where your residential is, and stuff like that. This is where your multi-units that's like a two-family flat and something that's four units and below. Now that's the left side of the quadrant, right? So you're dealing with the residential.

Now, where you start tapping into really making money is the right side of the quadrant: commercial, industrial, and land. Ultimately, you want to be playing this amazing real estate game from that right side. You can start on the left side of this quadrant, but the right side is where you start getting some really big numbers.

When I started, I was doing the residential thing. I met this guy who told me, "Kerry, if you want to make some real money, start investing in some commercials."

I said, "What do you mean real money?

He said, "Okay, you're making $20,000 here, you're making $5,000 profit, or maybe you make $50,000 profit here, but let me know when you're ready to make some real money." That's when he pushed me to get into the bigger game of investing.

I made my first purchase back in 2019 with a multipurpose commercial building. There were multiple units upstairs. There was a retail shop on the first level. And then, on the bottom level, it had a dance studio. This property I purchased for $75,000, and the after repair value was $450,000. And it didn't need much work; less than $100,000 worth of work. So that shows you I'm in a different ballgame.

So if you want to make some money, I will say that all my newbies start on the left side of the quadrant and learn at a small level. Once you learn the small level, you move to making big money–commercial and industrial.

Industrial buildings are the big warehouses that many manufacturing companies come in and buy. That's another game that I never tapped into, but other business partners of mine have, and I've seen them be very, very successful. These industrial properties don't take much rehab work. Generally, it's cleanouts. Maybe the roof leaks, so you may need to repair the roof, fix some garage doors, nothing crazy, you need to just prep the property and get it on the market to sell. Big manufacturing companies will come in and not just buy it, they may rent it from you. Now, if they buy it from me, we're talking a whole other story where you're going to make a lot of money depending on the square footage of that warehouse, and so on. Like I said before, on the right side of the quadrant is where you're going to make the majority of all your money— a lot of money in.

Let's move on to Land. So many ways you can go with land. You can clear off that land to sell to another developer. You can also get an architect, an engineer, and you can get some drawings done to pretty much create a vision for a developer. But before you do anything, you want to go down to the city to see what it's zoned for. Is it a commercial zone? Is it a residential zone? And based on that zoning, you can then map out what you want to put on that land, and then you can sell it, or you can just leave it clear to make a developer make those decisions on what they want to do.

I had land. I gave this land away to a deserving student of mine who gave me a proposal on what they would do with the land. This deserving student won the land for free. And I like to say free because they put in the work for it, so they deserved it. So that's the benefit of having land.

Now let's talk about wholesaling. This is how I started. Now, wholesaling is very popular with no money down, and it's important how you structure the deals with wholesaling. Like I told you before in my story, I started with someone else's money that I used to acquire this property. And then I was able to get the deed to give to that person who bought it from me. Wholesaling is a great strategy where you can put no money down, whatsoever, no money down. So wholesaling is very popular in the real estate business.

Let's talk about buy, fix, and flips. So the buy, fix, and flips may be in more of a low-income area. I like those areas because many people don't like to touch them. But to me, you have to have a vision in this business; you have to have a vision. And without vision, it is hard for you to see what it can become. So I'm a visionary. So when I see things, I look at them as they could be. I thought, *Oh, I can see the beautiful lawn. Oh, I could see the beautiful flowers. Oh, I could see the roof was done.* So you want to have a vision of looking past the bad stuff but looking at it in the future. A lot of my success in this business came because of my vision. I had a strong vision to see it in beautiful shape and beautiful condition.

Buy, fix, and flips are very popular because you're able to do the bare minimum to them. I will give you my strategy. What I do with the buy, fix, and flips is buy a property and put it in different categories. I would say this is tier one, this is tier two, and this is tier three. Let me explain.

Tier one: This is my top property. I do not want to buy and just sell as-is. I want to buy and put in high-end quality material to make it look more modern and attractive to a homeowner. So the tier ones are the properties that I sell to homeowners.

Tier two: Properties that I would do the bare minimum of fixing up because, let's be real, tenants do not take care of your properties. So you should not fix up a property for a homeowner and put a tenant in there because after a year, you're going to have holes in the wall, you're going to have things in the door, things are going to go wrong, I'll tell you that right now.

Another side note for you newbies is that when rehabbing these houses, do not put in carpet; go with hardwood floors. Either the original hardwood floors where you sand them down and stain them, or do vinyl flooring, whatever it is, do not do carpet. With carpet, every year, you have to go throughout that house and tear it out. That's a waste of money. So that's a side note.

Tier three: With my tier three deals, I do the bare, bare, bare minimum. What I mean by this is that the only thing that I do is prep it, I get it cleaned up, I get the yard cut, trees trimmed, and the walls may need to be scraped down. I make it look presentable enough that it gets an investor's attention. Keep in mind a lot of these properties people look past because they don't have the vision. So you have to create that vision for them and show them what it *could* be. So when they're going inside the house to do a walkthrough, they see that and understand this has potential.

I will give you a story about a property that I acquired for $2,000 in Detroit, Michigan. I bought the property for $2,000, and I wondered why nobody saw the potential in this property? I mean, it was a nice solid block. I mean, there were brick homes throughout the block. It was a nice solid block. It was probably the only house that was vacant on that block. As I said, I had the vision. So I began to develop more of my vision of how this property could become how I envisioned it. I hired a crew of laborers to trim the trees, cut the grass, and take off all the vines that grew on the house. So once we got the property cleaned up and got the doors put in, we made it look more presentable. Again, we did the bare minimum. We didn't do rehab. We just did a cleanup, and we added a nice door to the front and maybe scraped some of the walls down. It's like putting lipstick on a pig, right? We made it look presentable for another investor to see the potential. So did that work? Yes! Again, I bought it for $2,000, maybe put about a good $1,500 in, and then sold that same property for $15,000. Now that's the bare minimum. And that's what I call a nice buy, bare minimum fix, and a flip.

Let's talk about buy-and-hold single families. Now, personally, I don't just buy-and-hold. It can be a buy-and-hold strategy if you fix them up and put tenants in them, but my purpose is to sell these properties. The only ones that I like to keep are commercial properties. Commercial is what I like for my long-term wealth. Multi-unit residentials are fine to have, that's where I started, but I graduated from residential, the left quadrant, and went over to the big side of the quadrant, which is commercial and industrial. But if your strategy is to buy-and-hold, there are some benefits. Buy-and-hold single families are very important because these properties appreciate, especially if they are in a good community, a good district where it's going to hold its value; those are properties you want to hold.

Now I recommend that those who do a buy-and-hold have a house sitter in those properties or do the bare minimum to get Section 8 approved or a tenant approved with the city. So you can comply with all the city's rules, have an inspector come out there to inspect it to make sure that you're in good standing with the city as far as the codes. Make sure everything is up to code. When you buy a home, it doesn't make any sense to have it sitting there boarded up. You want to make some money out of it. So I will say if you're going to buy-and-hold, find ways to make money out of that property while you're sitting on it. Because I know some guys, even myself, did this as well, I sat on properties, and they became a liability, not an asset. I began to pay monthly insurance on these properties. I had to pay monthly maintenance for the upkeep of these properties. I started to get blight tickets (a violation for failing to maintain your property inside and out) and all types of things in the mail from the city, so that became a liability. So don't be like me; learn from me.

Now let's talk about the buy-and-hold multifamily. The buy-and-hold multifamily is what I love. I love buying multifamilies because you're making money day one, especially if you got this property rehabbed and fixed up. You have that income coming in, you're making some good money, and that's only going to appreciate. If you do decide to get a refinance on it, you're able to get a refinance up to, I believe, 65% loan to value. Now some of the lenders I know do up to 70% loan to value, but it depends on that private lending company or that bank institution what their terms are. But I know that you can get up to 70% loan to value on that property. So the money that you put in, you're getting that money back, your initial investment back, and you're allowing your tenants to pay that mortgage on it.

So the only way this thing will work is if you have qualified tenants. And what I mean by qualified tenants is someone who pays rent on time. One way to ensure that the rent is paid on time is to register your property as a Section 8 property. And I'll tell you one thing, the government pays on time and consistently. So I highly recommend that if you were to get into the buy-and-hold of a multi-unit, I would make that multi-unit Section 8 approved so that you can have Section 8 tenants in there to get that income consistently. That way, no one's taking a loss if a recession hits; this is recession-proof.

Alright, let's talk about a Real Estate Investment Trust (REIT). A REIT is a company that owns, operates, or finances income-generating real estate. Modeled after mutual funds, REITs pool the capital of numerous investors. This makes it possible for individual investors to earn dividends from real estate investment without buying, managing, or financing properties themselves. REITs can be attractive to investors who may not want to be hands-on in this business. I have not invested in it because I was doing my own thing. But for those that may want to get a start, to get a feel of what it is to invest, I would recommend getting into something like a REIT because you put your money somewhere, and you allow the experts to invest your money in real estate for you for a return. All these things will be agreed on before even starting. They will tell you what your terms are and what percentage you will get out of this return. And there are different levels to it. Some programs have it where you can invest as little as $1,000, $500, or even $100. So yeah, they have very diversified fund options for your investment in real estate.

Let's talk about Airbnb. Airbnb is the way to go right now. You know, this is how you evolve. You want to see how to maximize this real estate investment in your rental property. You may have a rental property that you may be looking to put a tenant in but just think about this. If you were to make your property into an Airbnb home, you're making five times the amount you would make with one individual tenant. So that one individual tenant, let's say, for example, that one individual tenant may pay you $800 a month. So $800 a month, that's only $800 a month. Now let's say you have 30 days to rent out this property, and you rented it out daily. If you rented this Airbnb home out for $150 a night, and every night you have this house booked up, that's $150 times 30, which comes out to $4,500. You have the potential to make $4,500 a month on this property. That's crazy compared to the $800 a month you would make with a traditional renter or tenant. Even if you don't rent the whole month out, let's say if you did 15 days out of the month, half of the month, that's $150 times 15, that's $2,250. So you catch my drift? You're making ten times as much money doing the Airbnb strategy. I think that's the new way; the new thing is Airbnb. They're taking over right now. Even those that don't own real estate property, you can structure a deal with that property owner, with the landlord, to permit you to sublease your property out or your unit out. You don't even have to own the property to rent out your apartment building. Do you think that sounds crazy? It's not crazy. It's smart.

CHAPTER 6

Building Your Team
(PTL Course)

When building a real estate investing team, you need ten team members essential to your success.

Number one: Mentor

Now, I found this to be very, very, very important. That's why it's number one. A mentor is very important because they can help guide you through every step of your success in your life, especially an experienced mentor who's in the field of what you're doing. A mentor is applied to everything in life. For example, if you're dealing with sports, what does a person have in sports? They have a coach.

When I was playing football, I had a coach that would tell me how to do this and how to do that, how I could develop my skills, and guide me and to watch over me and show like, "Yo, you're doing this wrong, Kerry, you need to do it this way." Do you know what I mean? So a coach is very important to have. This applies to everything in life. You need a coach. And a coach is a mentor.

So that's what I'm doing right now. As you're reading this book, I am coaching you to success because I'm telling you what you need to do and what you don't need to do, the dos and don'ts. So a mentor is someone who is going to guide you every step of the way to make sure you succeed in what you're doing. You're taking a shortcut to life in a way because you're taking these years of experience from this guy that is showing you the ropes, that's showing you the blueprint, the blueprint, that's what I like to say, the blueprint. So in this business, you want to make sure you have a real estate mentor.

Number two: Real estate attorney

Having a real estate attorney is important because you need to ensure that things are done right. You want to make sure that documents are looked over with your experienced real estate attorney. You want to make sure that not only documents are looked at, but you also want to make sure that you're doing title searches on these properties. And then you don't want to get caught up in the verbiage. Sometimes you can sign something without understanding the meaning. So it's really good to go over that contract with your real estate attorney whenever you are acquiring a property.

I didn't have a real estate attorney at the beginning of my real estate investing journey. I was just getting stuff off the internet, finding out how to do things, and talking to experienced people. But that's where I failed. That's how I got caught up in a lot of my failures. Because even though I was being mentored, there's only so much your mentor can do because he has to survive, he has to make money. So unless you're paying your mentor, he only has a certain amount of time actually to mentor you. A really good attorney will read the purchase agreement you may receive for the sale or the purchase.

Number three: Contractor

A contractor is important when you need to know the conditions of the properties you're acquiring. Before you make a nice offer, you want to be able to gather all this information about this property before you even submit an offer. For example, a property can be worth, let's say, $20,000 but needs $20,000 worth of rehab. It doesn't make any sense because the money you are putting in will be the value. So it's very important to see what the conditions are of that property so that you can make a reasonable offer because you're going to have a lot of surprises. So a contractor is very important to have. Especially if you're doing the fix and flips in this real estate business, you need a contractor who can give you the numbers of how much it will cost you to rehab the property.

Number four: Real Estate Agent

A real estate agent is a person who is licensed in that state to sell a property for you or to list properties for you. A typical commission percentage is 6%; 3% if it's someone else's deal and they split it with another agent.

Number five: Loan Officer

A loan officer deals with loans for your investment property. This is what I was speaking about earlier. Suppose you want to do a refinance (refi). In that case, you're going to need a real estate loan officer who can help you structure a deal to refi that property for a 60-75% loan to value. They can help you fill out the application and take you through that whole process of getting approved. And I have an affiliation with a mortgage company to help people get refinanced. I will share that with you guys in this book.

Number six: Title officer

A Title officer is someone at the title company who will help you with title searches, and also they will close properties at their facility. So a title company is very important because you need to submit your contracts which are your purchase agreements. They will be able to do all the work and put everything in a HUD statement to show what the buyer-side closing will be and what the seller-side closing will be. They also will issue you an owner's policy. You may want to get an owner's policy or warranty deed on that property. It's very important to get warranty deeds and not quitclaim deeds in this business because a quitclaim deed doesn't really mean anything.

The difference between a quitclaim deed and a warranty deed is with a quitclaim deed, there is no guarantee that the grantor is the rightful owner of the property in question. On the other hand, a warranty deed is a deed in which the grantor guarantees that they rightfully own the property and has the right to transfer it.

I highly recommend that anybody taking lessons from me stick to warranty deeds, not quitclaim deeds. I made my mistakes by getting quitclaim deeds that didn't mean anything. All a quitclaim deed tells that person is, I have no interest in this property. I'm giving all that interest to you. That's all the states. It's just conveying it over, conveying all the liens, conveying all the taxes, all the problems over to this individual or this entity. So that's why it's important to go the title company route and let them do their job and provide you with an insurance policy.

Number seven: Inspector

I like to put the inspector with the contractor. Because the city inspector will give the contractor a better idea of a quote for what needs to be done to the property and what the code requirements are. After an inspector comes out, they will put together this big, long sheet of things that need to be done to this property which can be given to the contractor to give you an accurate idea of what it's going to cost. So this inspector and the contractor will work hand-in-hand because it'll help him identify what needs to be fixed with that property, and he can give you a good honest quote. And going back to number three, the contractor, you don't want just one. You want multiple contractors to compare apples with apples and oranges with oranges. You want to make sure what this person is quoting is close or far off.

I have had experiences where three contractors come by. One gave me $5,000 below what the other person said, and the other one was $10,000 higher than everyone else. I was like, why is it such a huge difference? So you want to compare them so that the one you want to go with, you can bring their bid down by playing the contractors off each other. It's a bidding war to get the best deal. That's the secret that I want to share with you is how I'm able to negotiate the quotes for contractors. But we're talking about inspectors here. They are just there to show you what was wrong with the property and what needs to be done to the property so that way you can get that report and give it up to the contractor.

Number eight: Appraiser

While an inspector will tell you what needs to be done to the property to get it up to city code, an appraiser will tell you what type of improvements you should make to increase the property's value. An appraiser will tell you it's not important to finish out the basement, or it's no use to add an extra restroom when the comps are saying the houses in this area are going for this price without those additions.

Here's an example: my pastor had a property, and he gutted this house out to the studs. He put all the expensive, nice materials and stuff in there for a homeowner. He decided to finish the basement by adding a restroom, and he furnished it. It looked beautiful. I'm talking about an A-1, a very good quality home. He fixed up this house for a homeowner.

So after he fixed his house, the appraiser came by and asked why he spent the money to finish the basement? All these other houses are selling for $80,000 without a finished basement. So the comps showed that my pastor could only sell this property for $80,000. The only thing that finishing the basement might do is make the property more desirable for a homeowner to buy because it's like, "Oh, we got a full bathroom in the basement." It's going to help you sell it faster, but it's not going to change the numbers on what you're asking for.

So that was a lesson learned. I learned from it because I was supposed to advise him on certain things. After all, he can't be everywhere. He's a multimillionaire and has multiple entities, multiple businesses that he runs. So he trusted a couple of our team members and me to get the job done for him. We should have advised him like, "Sir, let's not do this, let's do this." That was how I learned we needed an appraiser on the team. The appraiser will show us how much money was put into it and how we need to design it as far as not adding the restroom or something like that, but just fixing this and fixing that.

I would advise the appraiser to communicate with the contractor because they all want to work hand-in-hand: the contractor, the inspector, and the appraiser.

Number nine: An Accountant

An accountant (CPA) is very important because he's the numbers guy. If you're working on a property, you want to see the numbers. You want to see your profit at the end. I made mistakes in my early investing by not documenting everything. I would just spend, spend, spend, spend to the point where when it came to tax time, I was trying to track down all the money that I paid into this property. I couldn't track down all the numbers. So I would take a big loss, and I had to eat that cost because I wasn't aware of how much I was putting into the property. An accountant will help you keep clean books and help you document all the expenses, so you're able to know what you actually profited at the end of the sale. So you can see how very important it is to have an accountant.

Number ten: Runner

You want to add a runner, boots on the ground, guy or girl. You need to create another you. And how you create another you is by having someone who assists you who will help you make the runs you need to make so you can focus on making money and keep bringing money in. Because if you're working in the business, and you can't get things done right, it will be an unorganized, chaotic organization. You want to make sure that you have a runner who can go to Home Depot, grab some stuff from the title company, check up on the contractors, or go downtown to pull some permits. Whatever it is, you need a runner on your team who will help assist you; you can call your runner your assistant. So number ten is very important.

So we talked about the ten members. We talked about a mentor. We talked about a real estate attorney. We talked about contractors. We talked about the real estate agent. We talked about the loan officer. We talked about the title officer, the title company. We talked about the inspector. We talked about the appraiser. We talked about the accountant. And we talked about the runner.

Now let me tell you how I found my team members. The mentor I found was based on his background and his proven success. I told myself this guy is a very successful businessman, and I want to be around that. So I found ways I could be around that, whether I needed to wash his car or if I needed to carry his briefcase to serve, wherever he needed help, I identified where his needs were, and I catered to that, and he became my mentor. Never look for a "hand out," but look for a "hand up." That's how opportunities come to you, is by giving a hand up and not having a hand out trying to always take from people. So you just have to give a little for you to receive a little. You reap what you sow. It's biblical principles; you reap what you sow. So the more you do these things, I'm telling you, it's a principle. And one thing about principles is when you implement them, principles will work.

I found the real estate attorney through a recommendation by the title company I was doing business with. I have more than one attorney because I'm doing so much. I want multiple things going on simultaneously at the same time. For instance, right now, I have one attorney looking over one set of my documents while another attorney is looking over my other deal, and he's trying to write up a purchase agreement that I'm going to send over to the buyer. A third attorney is doing a quiet title action on a property that needed clear title from my past mistakes of buying quitclaim deeds. So asking for a recommendation is a reliable way to find a good real estate attorney.

OK, let me give you the nuggets about how to find a contractor. So one of the ways I found a contractor was going to Home Depot. Ask yourself, where does every contractor go to buy materials? Home Depot. For instance, if you need a roof fixed, guess what department you need to go to? You need to go to the roofing aisle, where all the roofers are. That's how I found my roofing contractors. If I need some electrical work done, guess what I do? Not only do I go to the Home Depot electrical aisle, but I'll also go to other electrical stores where these electricians have accounts with. Because when you're dealing with certified and licensed contractors, they have accounts with these companies, and they get their materials at a discounted rate. So I would go to these stores to find an electrician and get contact numbers. I would say, "Hey man, my name is Kerry Lampkin, and I need to get a quote on a multi-unit or a residential unit." And I don't just get one name and number. I get multiple. I don't leave that Home Depot or that supply store until I get at least 20 people on my list of contractors in each category, from electricians to plumbers to whatever. So there's another of my secrets—Home Depot. You go to the aisle that's needed: the plumbing aisle if you need a plumber, the electrical aisle if you need an electrician, the lumber aisle if you are looking for a carpenter or someone who does framing work. That's how I found some of my guys. Many of them who still work for me to this day I found at Home Depot. Also pulling up to job sites. That's where you see a lot of action going on. I'd pull up to the job sites and get their numbers as well. So that's how you find your contractors.

For a real estate agent, you can simply use recommendations or find them through Google searches. I searched the web for real estate agents, and I interviewed them. I asked questions like, how long have you been a real estate agent? How well do you know the market? What are your recent sales? Whatever it is, you can interview them to know if this is the individual you want to go with. So do a Google search and go from there. You can also utilize your social media to find a real estate agent. Because one thing about real estate agents is that they are trying to get their stuff out there, the things they have under contract. They need that publicity. They need to put their stuff out there so that way they can make a sale. So it's easy to find these real estate agents by the web or social media and by doing your homework on them.

How do you find a loan officer? The same way you find a real estate agent. Google search or social media. In whatever city you're in, if you're in Michigan, loan officers in Michigan; or if you're in Texas, a loan officer in Texas, whatever city you're in, loan officers in Detroit, Michigan, loan officers in Atlanta, Georgia, you know. So whatever it is, you'll find loan officers and brokers on the web and through the title company's recommendations. Because think about it, the title company deals with many individuals. They deal with investors. They deal with loan officers. They deal with banks. They deal with attorneys. They have so many resources at the title company. I would ask the title company owner, "Hey, do you know anybody that can help me with my books?" or a good accountant? Or you know, a real estate attorney he could recommend me to? Or, "Hey, you know some contractors?" Yes, even contractors, I'm telling you. You'd be surprised what information the title company has.

Let's go to number seven, the inspector. How do you find the inspector and add them to your team? Find the inspector's office in your city. For example, for my properties in Detroit, Michigan, I go to the

WHY REAL ESTATE & WHY NOW?

Building and Safety Department in the Coleman Young Building. The Building and Safety Department on the fourth floor is where you get an inspector. You will have to fill out an application with the property information, pay a fee, and then set up a schedule with one of the city inspectors to come out there to inspect the property. So finding an inspector is simply going to your local city downtown to request an inspector to come out. So however their system is, you just have to follow those rules.

Next is the appraiser. I found the appraiser through word of mouth. I asked my loan officer, "Hey, Tom, do you have any appraisers?" As a loan officer, he deals with appraisers all the time because he gives out loans. Banks need to know, "What does this property appraise for?" So he gave me the name and number of the appraiser the bank uses and, Boom! I got my appraiser. You can also simply use Google.

Number nine was an accountant. Now, I'm very big on who oversees my money, so I like recommendations from people I know. I reached out to my pastor, one of my mentors in the real estate business, and my spiritual father. I know that he had a trusted source, the people who watched over his funds. I weighed who he sent me and another person who I was researching from another source, a trusted source. So I decided who I would use by relying on people I trusted. Again, it's important to get a recommendation from someone in your circle, someone you're connected to, who is probably currently using a CPA they trust. Go with a trusted source when you're dealing with your finances.

And finally, the runner. This may take some interviewing on your part. I found my runner by trusting some of the guys in the city who needed work. I would always try to look at who would fit this job description. Are they smart? Do they know how to adapt? Do they know how to read the temperature in the room? I would literally just work with them, work around them, and then decide on the best person to go with. I always pick individuals who are good with people who know how to talk and how to treat people right and not let their authority go to their head because your runner is a representation of you. So if he goes out there and does something wrong, it's going to look like you are doing something wrong. Just use your best judgment, utilize your brain to make the best decision.

Now, I'm calling them a runner, but really they are your assistant. Make sure that person has transportation. I made a mistake early in my investing career of hiring an assistant who didn't have a car. He didn't have a debit card or bank account set up; it was like I was his dad. You don't want to be anybody's daddy or mommy. Just make sure that they're responsible individuals that can do this work for you. They have their own transportation, their own bank accounts set up, and things like that. So that's how I found my ten team members.

Let's talk about how time is money—money is time. You want to make sure you're maximizing your day. It's very important to maximize your day. And how you maximize your day is by eliminating all distractions and learning to delegate. As I discussed with the ten team members, I delegate many things to my runner. You have to organize your business and structure things the right way if you want your business to grow.

One of my mentors told me that you can literally grow yourself out of business. And what I mean by this is you can be growing so much, and without a foundation, without team members in place, your business will crash; your business will shut down because you don't have any order.

One of the ways that I can help you in this book is by creating instructions on how to have order in your business. First, eliminate all distractions. I'm talking about everything, anything that doesn't help or benefit your business or what you're doing. Cut it off and focus on one "plant" at a time. Because if you have multiple "plants" growing that you're watering, it's hard to water everything. You must focus on that business, that "plant," and give it all your attention and water it, so you can watch it grow.

Learn to delegate. Delegate some of your responsibilities to your runner so that person can help you organize and keep things operating. Don't work *in* your business. You have to be *in control* of your business where you're delegating things for your workers to do. One of the mistakes I made early on was working in my business. I was helping contractors by doing Home Depot runs. I was driving here and there. I had a dumpster company, and I was driving a dumpster truck. I was going to the landfill. I was answering phones. I was doing everything, and I thought I was doing the right thing. But I was doing the wrong thing because I was not delegating that. It took a lot of my time, and I lost a lot of money.

I could've been making more money with my time if I had delegated that. I needed to eliminate myself from driving the truck. I had to eliminate my answering the phones; I have an answering service. I had to eliminate making Home Depot runs; the runner's doing that now. So that's what I mean about distractions. All that was distractions for me growing my business because I was in the mix. I was *in* the business. You just have to be very smart about it. You don't want to be in the business. You want to delegate the business so you can do more things and make more money.

Lastly, with this chapter, I want you to remember that more is given to those who have been a good steward of what you have. In this real estate business, when you start making money, you start accumulating properties, you start gaining more wealth, you always want to remember that being a good steward is the secret to this, which is being a good manager over all the things that interest you. Being a good manager allows more doors to open up for you.

Everything that I mentioned is all management. Everything I mentioned about building your team in this chapter teaches you how to be a good manager because now you oversee these departments. So every ten team members you have, see it as a department, right? And you're overseeing each one of those ten departments, and you're delegating. You want to be able to look in from the outside and say, "How's it going over here?" When you're delegating, and you're managing, things will run smoothly.

Have you guys ever noticed how more is given to those who have? My theory is they are great managers. When other people who have true wealth see something done in a certain order that's organized, they are attracted to that. Wealth is attracted to management. Remember that—wealth is attracted to management.

Once I got this managing thing down, and I got this structure thing in order, I started seeing more wealthy people, very successful people, be more attracted to me because they thought, *This guy's work ethic, this guy's doing something right.* Believe it or not, people who have true wealth know when someone else is doing something right. In the streets, we call it "real recognizes real." Do you know what I mean? Bosses recognize bosses. Wealthy people recognize wealthy people. They know he's a young king, or she's a young queen, that if you get this thing down, you will prosper. This is one of the key principles to your success is being a good steward over what God has entrusted you with.

If you have these things in place, you will be successful, and you won't fail. The only way you will fail is if you skip the process. I just told one of my students, "Look, you can't skip the process. You have to go through the process." I broke it down to her. I told her that nothing escapes the law of process. And I told her to write it down as a note. These are principles that I'm giving you. And if you skip any one of these laws or you skip any one of these principles, that's when you will see things not flow how you want. Everything I'm telling you is how I learned from my experiences and failures.

CHAPTER 7

Finding the Deals

I have multiple ways to find deals in a buyer's market and seller's market. I like to be boots on the ground because I like to get a feel for an area whenever I'm driving. I will always keep my head on a swivel, looking for a deal. I've developed an eye for noticing overgrown grass and a roof that needs repair, things like that. I've found a lot of deals in real estate that way.

Let's start with my buyer's list and seller's list of people who reached out to me to purchase one of the properties I had listed. I then begin to build an actual list of investors and a list of sellers and wholesalers. Many deals come to me by just staying in communication with the people who reached out to me in the past. In my very first deal that I did, I relisted an ad on Craigslist and took better photos, and even maintained the yard a little better where I made it look presentable when I reposted it. The guy I bought the property from had it on Craigslist with a simple, blurry, Google Maps photo. I went boots on the ground, got the address, and went by there and saw that this property had a lot of potential. It just wasn't being presented in the best way. Presentation rules everything. You have to make sure you take great photos when listing the property.

I also find properties by harnessing the power of the internet. The internet is so good for deal searching in a buyer's market. For example, I did hashtags, #Detroitrealestate, #Detroitmultiunits, #Detroitapartment-buildings. The reason why I'm saying Detroit is because that's where I started investing very, very heavily, and literally, these properties were pennies on the dollar. It was like a great place for a newbie like myself to get started. I wasn't even putting any of my own money into my first deals. I just put a little bit of sweat equity, some time into it, and some faith and some work behind it.

What to look for in a deal. It depends on the type of deal that you're seeking. One thing that I look for in a deal is if there will be enough room for me to profit and the investors to profit. I don't buy a deal if there's not a good profit margin. I don't like that type of deal. Especially if I negotiate with the seller and the seller doesn't want to budge on his price. It's not worth it. I look for deals with big profit margins. Here's an example. The property may be worth $150,000, and it probably needs about a good $20,000 worth of work, and the seller only wants $50,000. Whoa! You have yourself a nice little deal where it's enough for your investor to make money as well. Because all in, if you look at it this way, the $150,000 divided by the $70,000 that you have to put into it—$50,000 for purchases and the $20,000 for rehab—you have an $80,000 profit margin in there on this deal. That's more than a 50% return, and that's a great deal. Depending on the investor's preferences, some may be happy with a 10%, 15%, or 20% return, so the more profit you have in the property, the better. Those are the types of deals that I'm seeking.

Next is to make sure that you have an exit strategy going into the deal. As I've mentioned earlier, you always want to do your due diligence before moving forward with any deal. You want to make sure you get the basic information such as where it's located, how much they want for it, and what condition it is in before you get too deep into pulling title work and all that. So you want to exit before you enter so you don't waste your time, and you don't spend all this money not knowing what you're fixing this thing up for. Are you fixing it up for a tenant? Are you fixing it up for a homeowner? Or are you fixing it up just to do the bare minimum and sell to another investor. You have to know what you're getting into before getting into the deal. So exit before you enter.

Next, we're going to talk about researching the marketplace. Where should you invest? What are you looking for in a marketplace? I like to look for multi-units because I've graduated to another level of investing in bigger real estate. For my newbies, I recommend you start on a smaller project such as a residential property so that way you could then learn as you go. Hopping into something like a multi-unit right away could be a little challenging. I'm not telling you not to do it, but having a 15 unit apartment building is like having 15 individual houses, especially if they need work done to it. So keep that in mind. You can start big and earn big, but you could also lose big when you start big. So you want to get an understanding about it before getting into that. Let's get back to researching the marketplace. When researching, look for multi-units because multi-units are recession-proof. I believe people like to downsize to something affordable whenever they lose a job, whenever they may get a pay cut. Recently, people losing their jobs due to COVID has caused them to downsize. It forced them to come up with another game plan for their lifestyle. I've seen it happen over and over again. So guess where those people were running to? They were running to the multi-units. And to me, I think that's a good safety net when it comes to investing in multi-units.

Another benefit of having a multi-unit is having everything in one location. If you have a 15 unit property, all the units are in one place. You don't have to run across town, back and forth to different properties. It's all in one place, which makes maintenance easier. There may be a cost to having a runner or assistant drive around all day to different locations, so consolidating all their work to a multi-unit saves you money. That's why I'm in the multi-unit business. We'll talk more about that later.

So what are you looking for in a marketplace? I've already mentioned my preference for multi-units. Often you have these investors who want to own the property for two years and then sell the property based on the cap rate. I like those types of deals too because it's already performing, and you don't have to go through the headache of buying something vacant, putting rehab money into it, and then managing it. There's so much to it, so much time in managing and money spent. The best option is to find a property that is already performing because the person who had it before you went through the headache already; they did the hard part. You may pay a little bit more money, but it's worth it because these properties appreciate over time, so you're not losing money. You have an asset, something that's bringing money to you, not taking from you.

Next, I want to talk about what tools I use. My favorite tool, the best tool to use as an investor, is called PropStream. PropStream is software that helps you get details about a property. It helps you find the recent sale. It helps you find who the owners are. You can do a skip trace that allows you to get the information on the owner.

Another thing I love about it is you can see how much they paid for that property. That'll help you negotiate the price down, especially if they haven't put any work into it. You're able to see that they only paid $10,000 for the property and didn't do any rehab work on it. You can offer $15,000 and see if they take it. You never know because they may be at a point where they need to sell it. Maybe they are in a situation where they got a better deal and would like to take the cash out of it and put that money towards their bigger deal. You just never know. So PropStream has allowed me to move a lot faster than when I started, when I was driving by properties writing addresses down, going to the Coleman Young building, or the Wayne County treasurer's office where they do your search for who owns the property on the deed. Think about everything that goes into this. You have to pay $5 to print the paperwork out when you go downtown. Why waste time spending the money, trying to find a parking spot, waiting in line for the kiosk machine to print the stuff out. It's time you can use more effectively. PropStream helped me work smarter and not harder.

Let's talk about the internet, how I could harness its power when researching properties, and all the information I talked about in PropStream. I have a saying, "Doing the do." Doing the do encompasses everything in the PropStream software. You're able to find who the owner is or find out the company name. Before I discovered this PropStream app, I would go to the Secretary of State's website. In Michigan, it's called LARA (Licensing and Regulatory Affairs). That's where you get your business licensing. Whether it's real estate, LLC, liquor, all types of stuff, you get your business license from the Secretary of State. So with PropStream, I would get the information about this person or company, and I would go to the Secretary of State's website and type that information into the business entity search bar. You'd be surprised what pops up when you put in that individual's name. All of the businesses that person is affiliated with, even if he's doing joint ventures or a registered agent, anything that's tied to that LLC or company name, will pop up, and that's one of the ways I package the whole thing. Because I don't want to know a little bit about an individual, I want to know everything. I want to know how long they've been in business, how long they have been in real estate, and when the company was formed. This allows me to feel more comfortable doing business with this person because I see they have successful businesses. This will give you peace of mind if you would like to do business with that person based on what you discovered through your due diligence.

I recently did my due diligence on an individual who wanted to partner with me, which would cost me about $50,000. So I started looking into this individual because he said he's been in business for quite a long time. I came to find out he had 12 entities that were dissolved. He's been doing this since 2005 and dissolved his last company in 2019. That right there showed me this person is not all the way legit. Do you know what I mean? This raised a red flag to not do business with him at all. So this will help you discover who you're dealing with once you start doing your due diligence.

CHAPTER 8

Finding the Money

There are a lot of ways to find the money. And just know that there's always a solution to the problem. There's never a problem. There's always a solution when it comes to finding money.

The right strategy accumulates cash from wholesaling upfront to do deals. Here's an important point. If you live in an area where you grew up all your life, you know the good side of town, you know the bad side of town, it gives you an advantage as an investor, because you know about that area. So you're able to determine a good deal if you find a property with potential with great comps in a certain area or district. You know you can acquire that property at a certain price, knowing it has value to wholesale to another investor. The real key to wholesaling is to try to buy low and sell high. You get the property at a lower price and then sell it at a higher price with enough wiggle room that you make an acceptable profit even if they negotiate.

Always remember when negotiating, you want to start with a high price so that even if there is some haggling and counteroffers from the other investor, you're still able to comfortably agree on a mutual price that gives you the profit you hope to make on the sale.

So to go back to the strategy on how to accumulate cash from a wholesaling deal where you avoid coming out of the deal with no money, you have to make sure that you and the seller are in great communication. The seller has to have an agreement with you before you even pitch this property for sale. So you want to make sure that you have an understanding with the seller, and you do your due diligence to make sure that the property can sell for the price that you're asking. That's why I mean the total package of knowing what the comps are, the condition, and how much it will cost for the rehab. That way, you can factor in those numbers to help you give him an offer. Having that total package together also helps convince that investor that he's getting a good deal.

For example, the strategy that I used for one of my properties was, I looked at the condition, I knew that it needed some yard work, the inside of the property wasn't as bad, it just needed some lovin', and some minor repairs and things like that. I wanted to make this property look more presentable. This is part of my strategy. I cut the grass. I trimmed some trees. It didn't cost me much because I own a lawnmower and the cutters. I bought some trash bags, and I put that stuff on the curb for the trash man to pick up. Again, I found this property on Craigslist, and it was a bit of a mess. So when I reposted it on Craigslist, after making it look more presentable, I had over 20 people who reached out to me wanting to buy this property from me. I listed it for $10,000. I had some people offering me $5,000; some people offered me $7,000. But I took the biggest offer, which was $10,000.

So with that being said, I locked the contract in with the guy. I made a purchase agreement with the seller. I told the seller to give me 15 to 30 days to close. Now I know that it wasn't guaranteed I'd close in 15 to 30 days, but just know that I had it in my mind to close a deal to make something happen. I was sure that it was going to sell. I made it presentable. And the main thing is you just have to close people out. You have to present your proposal well. That's what you're doing. You're presenting this proposal to the buyer, and you let them know you have this beautiful property here for sale, etc. You have to make this thing very desirable for them to even bite on it. So that's what I did. I made it very desirable. I took nice pictures from different angles, reposted it online, and got over 20 calls. The guy that was interested offered me $10,000. I then told him to give me $1,000 as an earnest money deposit (EMD). I used that EMD to pay for the property from the original seller out of state in California. He overnighted me the deed. Once the deed was in my name, I could then deed it to the new buyer, the $10,000 guy.

We closed on a private sale at the actual property. And the guy gave me cash. Before our meeting, I prepared the deed on my computer, printed it out, and got it notarized. I asked the guy for his name and other information from the purchase agreement. I got all that on the purchase agreement. So I was able to write that information on the deed. Once I got all the information plugged in, I took it to a notary who put a little stamp on it. I met this guy at the property, we exchanged the money, I gave him the deed, and that's how I was able to complete my first deal without any of my own money. I did that 12 more times because the person I bought the property from had 12 more residential properties. We did more deals because he had some industrial buildings he wanted to sell that I sold as well. Even though I had the money, I didn't use my own money. I put my money in the savings because I knew I might need it to do future deals. After I got my first $100,000 in less than three months, I was able to be in the game to invest in properties and rehab properties. So, that's how you strategize, find money, and get money based on what I experienced.

Personal Capital:

Some people may have money saved, but I recommend investing money, not saving money. I read an article one time with Mark Cuban, the owner of the Dallas Mavericks. When asked about the value of saving vs. investing, Cuban recommended, "Once you're able to save [for] a year of expenses, then you can start investing and putting it into something that can appreciate."[3] In simple terms, put your money to work for you by investing it. And there are different levels to this too. If you don't have the full amount, there are different investments you can get into without having to put your time into it. You can put money in on a project for a return. You can go to trusted sources that do crowdfunding and things like that. They have private and accredited investor sides, where you have to be accredited to invest. So if you make over a certain amount a year, which is over $200,000 a year, or if you have over a million dollars in assets, you are an accredited investor. You can join groups like that which can offer you a nice return on your money.

The next thing you can do is utilize your credit. If you don't have business credit, you can start with your personal credit. This is a great strategy because there are different funding options available for those with a credit score of 650 and above; especially if you are low 630 and above, there are great opportunities. The interest may not be as good, but it's a good start. Don't look at it as debt but as an investment. Because there is such a thing as good debt, and there's such a thing as bad debt. Good debt is something that you utilize to bring money back in. You're using that debt to buy assets that make you wealthier, make you rich. Credit is what makes you rich. Credit is everything. Credit is your life.

---

[3] https://www.cnbc.com/2020/09/14/mark-cubans-top-financial-advice.html

I have business partners who use their business credit for everything. I used to be against it. I was told growing up that piling up your credit card is bad for you because those people didn't have a business plan; they didn't have an exit strategy. They were buying liability things such as cars, clothes, and things like that, luxury things that didn't bring any money in; it was taking money out of them, and that's when you get into debt. If you spend money on a credit card and you don't have any income coming in from an investment, it's just stupid—it's dumb.

I see what Mark Cuban says about saving; saving doesn't do anything. And the bank doesn't even pay that much interest. What do you get, 1% or 0.5% for keeping your money in their account? Just know that investing your money is the best way to do it.

Family and Friends:

You can utilize family and friends, but know that this can be risky. I don't use family just for the sake of keeping the peace. I don't recommend doing business with family because I've heard stories about people falling out based on money situations. It can get ugly, as you can imagine. So just know that family and friends are a source you can use, but be very wise about those decisions.

I think a lot of what goes wrong when trying to invest with a family or borrow money from a family member or a friend is not having things in writing. I will give you an example. In my family, we all have some land that we own together. There are 12 of us who pitched in to buy this very nice piece of property right off the highway. We use this property to sell fireworks every year: 4th of July and New Year's. We bought the land as a family, but one thing that we didn't do is that we didn't put it in writing. We also have more land in that same area that's been passed on verbally. My great-grandpa told my grandpa that when he dies, that land is his, and so on down the line it goes. But nothing has ever been put in writing. There isn't proper documentation to make it right, to put it in black and white. I think that could be a reason why family and friends may fall out. You think it is your family, so you trust them like "we good," but this is business. You have to do business the right way. Do it correctly. When you do it correctly, it doesn't come back to hurt you in the future. If, for instance, this person died, and now you have to do some type of clearing up of the title on the probate or whatever it is because you didn't have things properly done in the beginning.

So for those reading this, you want to make sure not only to do your due diligence, but the main thing is doing things correctly and doing things right. When you do the hard things first, later on in life, it is easier. That's where my family failed at owning this land. To this day, we still don't have the proper documents because my grandpa and my great uncle have both passed away. We have this land, but no one has the right documentation. So I took the initiative to hire an attorney to get it corrected.

If you decide to invest with family and friends, you want to make sure that you fill out and sign the right documents to avoid confusion. You have it in writing if you forget, was it 50% ownership when someone else thought it was 60/40. It's in black and white. Whatever is notarized and recorded is what's recorded; you both signed off on it. You need to have an operating agreement with friends, family, or investors. There always has to be some sort of operating agreement, so if there's ever an issue, you have the terms of what was agreed upon.

Other People's Money: Such as joint venture partners.

With a joint venture, you may decide to do a 50/50 split with an individual. You may not even have the money, but you have an idea. So in exchange for your idea, if a partner brings the funds, you can do a 50/50 partnership. Keep in mind that person may not think it's fair to do 50/50 because they are funding the project. They may feel like without them, there is no deal. So be open to negotiating and take a lower percentage if it gets the deal done. Once you start making money, you can do these deals on your own. So keep in mind that you don't have to have the funds to make it happen, but you want to make the deal pleasing for your partner. If it's a 60/40 split, you take 40. If it's a 70/30, you take 30. At the end of the day, if you make this guy or girl money, they're going to want to continue to be your investor; you can do bigger projects with them. So it's all about building relationships when you're in this thing. So joint ventures are very good. Joint ventures and partnerships are ways you can find money and get deals done.

Pitch Deck: (A pitch deck presentation is a visual document that provides investors with essential information about your business plan).

The Pitch Deck offer is something that I use when I need funding. When I don't want to use my own funds, I use investors' funds. With a pitch deck, you have to have all the details: what their percentage will be, what will it cost, and what will the percentage be on their return on investment? Is there equity involved? All the details must go inside of this. What you're doing is you're giving them your vision because sometimes it's hard to say things over the phone or in a meeting. But when you have that pitch deck, you're able to walk them through your plan when you're trying to sell them something.

Think of the TV show *Shark Tank* when deals are presented to the Sharks. Business owners have one shot at presenting their idea and doing it right. They demonstrate how their product works. They demonstrate what it looks like. They show it to them. They may even give them samples: feel, touch, see this, taste this, whatever it is. That's their pitch. They're pitching their business to get money. Unfortunately, a lot of them fail because their pitch wasn't effective.

One of the biggest reasons people fail in this business is that their pitch didn't make sense when it came to numbers. Make sure you know your numbers. It's like *Shark Tank*. Some people don't get the backing they want because their numbers aren't right. That's the biggest key. Because let me tell you, dealing with these investors, I've learned what matters to them is numbers. If you don't have numbers, just forget it. They may listen to what you say but then pat you on the back and say goodbye. Don't guess and give them projections of what they could make. No, be sure about it, be confident about it, and know your market. Everything should be in that pitch deck: what're the comps? Are you generating money from it now? What have you made? What's your experience like? Have everything in that pitch deck to win them over. That's another way to get money from investors without using your own money.

Hard Money:

Hard money is something that I would stay away from if you have other funding sources. Hard money should be your last resort, your last option. The simple reason is that the interest rates on these loans are a killer. I did hard money loans just as a way of building the relationship. I didn't need it at the time, but just in case I got in a pinch because of all the properties I was working on, I wanted to build a relationship.

I'm giving you some strategy right now. This is a secret. I'm giving you the Golden Nugget here. If I were to build relationships with multiple private lenders and hard money lenders and investors, I would have them in my back pocket if I ever needed them. And it worked. I did have times when I needed them to help me with a big deal that I was doing.

One deal I did, I used a hard money lender. I had a multi-unit; it was a multipurpose use. It had retail, a dance studio, and it had apartments upstairs. Man, it was nice and in a great location. So what I did was I got $75,000 from this guy, and he was charging me crazy interest. It was like 17%, and he was charging by the month. Each month, on that $75,000, I had to pay him. So it was like paying a mortgage.

Now, I had a bigger deal, and I used a portion of those funds for the bigger deal. I didn't want to disclose that bigger deal to them because they would have wanted more money out of me. Once I sold the bigger deal, I used that money to pay his loan off. And the success of that, them making 17% interest off me a month and then paying the initial investment that they gave me back plus 17% interest, that was a game-changer for me. I thought, *this guy's good, I want to invest more with him.* So now I got to where they were trying to throw money at me. They were asking, "You got another deal? You got another deal?" So it was expensive money to use, but I was able to do the bigger deal, and, to this day, I still have that hard money lender in my back pocket. I mean by back pocket, I have their contact information, and I have them on standby if I ever need them for a future deal. I plan on using these hard money lenders for my students who may not have money. So if you join my group, I will direct you in the right direction to get hard money lending.

So I gave you the game on the hard money lender. So that's a strategic plan. You can use that for other things too. You can use that with your joint venture partners or with an investor. You can utilize that with your family and friends. So that same strategy that I did, that I strategically planned out to get money to build that relationship with the hard money lenders, you can do the same thing with the other lenders, whoever you get money from, so that you can build that relationship. But you have to have a plan because you will lose their money if you don't have an exit strategy and a plan. That worked for me because I had a plan and an exit strategy.

Bank's Money:

Your loan officer will be able to help you with the bank's money. I have an affiliate link with this private lender company that gives mortgages for refinances or investment loans. So if an investor wants to buy a property that's performing, or if the investor wants to buy a vacant property, or an investor wants to buy land, it is this company called Heart Mortgage. They gave me an affiliate link, and it shows me how many people signed up underneath me, and I get a commission on this as well. So make sure you click on the link to go directly to the page if you want to help. Because with the funds that I get from these guys, I use these funds to help expand my brand and to use it to teach it to you, like this book that you're reading, this book is going towards the cost of getting this information out. For more information regarding private lending, hard money lending, and business credit, visit my website at KerryLampkin.com.

The next thing I want to talk about is **lines of credit**. I have three lines of credit right now. I have a line of credit with a private lending company. I have one that's for $640,000, another for $100,000, and a third for $250,000. I don't use them right now. But they are there if I need them. It's good to keep this in your back pocket because you never know how things will go. Money comes and goes, and it's a roller coaster when dealing in business. So it's good to have these lines of credit for future deals.

For those of you reading this book and needing additional consulting and information, join our student group. For more information on finding money, go to KerryLampkin.com.

CHAPTER 9

Doing the Deal, Putting All the Pieces of the Puzzle Together

S o you got the money, and you found your deal, now what? First, you want to make sure that you follow your plan. You also want to make sure that with the ten team members you put together that you make sure you oversee them. Do not put your trust and faith in it because we're all human; we all make mistakes. And sometimes, as humans, we do drop the ball at times. I've learned this through experience to ensure that I oversee all departments, no matter how big or small. Make sure that you have everything in place because you're dealing with other people's money. You want to treat this as if it is your money. This is your baby. You don't want to mess up relationships within a day. It's a small world. If you lose some investor money because you don't know what you're doing, people won't want to do business with you again, and they will talk about you with other investors. You don't want that. So you want to make sure you do everything in your power to make this deal successful.

That's what I had to do. I had to make sure when I was dealing with their money, I was on point with it. I want to make sure that I'm overseeing every department and know where everything, every penny, is going because everything has to be accounted for. Make sure you're putting everything together, all the pieces to the puzzle.

Let's talk about making an offer. As I've mentioned several times, you have to do your due diligence before making an offer: what's the condition? How much is the rehab? Are there unpaid back taxes? Everything has to be accounted for. You have to know everything.

Remember when I mentioned in the last chapter about knowing numbers. You have to know your numbers when making an offer because this is how you can negotiate the deal. You negotiate the deal by looking at that profit margin after doing the math and adding everything up. This is the after-repair value. This is what needs to go into it, and this is what we could sell it for to a homeowner or an investor. Some investors buy it at homeowner prices to put qualified tenants in there. The benefit of finding investors like that is that they have money and want to do a 1031 exchange, so they don't have to pay taxes on money going into a hard asset. So again, you can't make a reasonable offer if you don't know your numbers and what's all wrong with that property. Once you get the numbers, you can make an offer and negotiate the deal.

How I do it is once I gather all the information, I see what all needs to go into this property, I will then submit an offer form, and we'll go back and forth. Sometimes they're insulted by your offer, and sometimes they're like, "Let me think about it." You never want to go into a deal looking and sounding desperate. That kills your deals. Being desperate kills your deals. I never was a desperate person when I was trying to negotiate and make an offer or even sell a property. I never sound desperate because I know that would make me want to walk away from a deal. I always carry myself in a professional way. But it's important to remember that your offer is your offer. When you make that offer, try to give them a day or two. For example, you may tell them, "I'll give you $35,000 for your deal."

And they may say, "Man, $35,000 is too low. I was asking for $50,000. Why $35,000?"

I can then explain to them since I know about all the pieces, I know about all the details of this property, the condition, what the taxes are, knowing what my closing costs are going to be, all the expenses I'm looking at, it's going to cost about to get $15,000-$20,000 to rehab.

So now they're shaking their head and saying, "Okay, can I get back to you in 24 hours? Let me sleep on it."

Give them 24 hours to sleep on it. Make sure you follow up with them within those 24 hours but don't be hitting them back, "Oh, did you make a decision, did you make a decision?" don't sweat the deal. Just let him respond because he may need the money, or he may need to move on to the next market or next investment. He may also just be very motivated to sell the property.

So you want to make sure you're not desperate when making an offer or negotiating a deal. You want to put your poker face on. You don't want them to know what you have in your hand. You want them to feel like they need you, not the other way around. So that goes with my strategy for negotiating a deal: you know your stuff, you know the numbers, and you are very stern about what you're willing to give them, what you're willing to offer them.

So we've talked about you making an offer, what about you making a sale? With you having a property for sale, you want to make sure when you negotiate, you're also being very stern on your asking price. Again, you want to make sure that you're not looking or sounding desperate because people will prey on your needs. I know this because I'm an investor myself. I know how to size someone up and know that they are in desperate need because they just won't say no. You can see the desperation all over them.

When you're negotiating a deal with another investor for a property you have under contract or own outright, you want to make sure that you stay true to your numbers. But you also want to make sure that it is fair enough for them to make money. You can't say the after repair value is $175,000, and after doing all the repairs, you want every little bit of $175,000. Have some wiggle room. Because at the end of the day, any profit is good profit to me. Don't be greedy—greed kills deals. Especially if you have a nice profit margin, don't go too extreme with it. You want to go ahead and sell if the offer is there. Sell, if you can, because you want to move on to the next deal. Each day your money is not making money for you is not good. So you want your money to make money for you. So make your money and move on to the next deal.

That's part of doing the deal and putting all the pieces of the puzzle together. You want to make sure you get all the detailed information about that property to make a better offer, or you can negotiate the price to the price you want it for, a reasonable price.

Let's talk about the contracts you need and how to use them: assignment agreement, purchase agreement, lease agreement, and transactional close agreement.

Number one: Assignment agreement

An assignment agreement is really for wholesalers. It allows you to lock in a property as a wholesaler. They are commonly called assignment fees. So the assignment fee allows you to sell your assignment or a property that you have found, and you're helping that seller sell their property. You already have a list of buyers willing to buy assignments, so this is your commission. Your assignment agreement is like a flat fee. Both parties sign this agreement. And please know that they will know how much you're making, whether it's $5,000 or $10,000; most assignment fees are around that amount. You don't want to stack too much on there because it'd be harder for you to sell. And as investors, we know that you have to make money too because you can't be working for free. So the assignment agreement simply states what you're going to get out of this property for helping that buyer find a property or helping that seller sell their property. Whenever you're closing at a title company, all these documents are submitted to the underwriter at the title company. And they will then put the HUD statement together so that when they close, the seller can see the HUD statement, and the buyer can see the HUD statement to see what all money is taken out and what all money needs to be paid to the title company in escrow.

That's the extent of my knowledge of the assignment agreement. I'm going to be completely honest with you, I have never done an assignment agreement. I knew about it, but I skipped the process because I wanted to make more money on my certain deal, and I didn't want to disclose how much I was making off of these deals. I'm talking about some deals I made $100,000. Imagine if I put that on the assignment fee agreement that I want $100,000, and I'm getting this property for $20,000, and I'm selling that thing for $120,000. The sellers are going to be like, "You've screwed me. You ripped me off. You got over on me." Or they're going to want more money from me. So that was the reason why I didn't want to do assignment agreements because I didn't want to disclose the amount of money I was making. Think about it, both sides are going to be upset. Your seller will be upset, and the buyer's going to think he's been ripped off because he paid $120,000 for something he could have got for $20,000 to $50,000. Do you see what I'm saying? He would have been able to negotiate it lower based on seeing my contract and the amount of money I was making.

Number two: Purchase agreements

Purchase agreements include everything agreed upon between the buyer and seller, from the purchase price to everything that comes with that property. Everything must be put into that purchase agreement. Who will be paying for taxes, the seller or the buyer? If there's an outstanding water bill for $500, who's paying for that? Everything needs to be worked out and agreed upon before the property can close. Because the title company will not cut any checks or unless that water bill or back taxes, all that has to be paid.

So make sure everything you have verbally agreed on is written into that purchase agreement: the purchase price, the disclosures, is there lead in the property? Etc. I advise you to have a real estate attorney go over that purchase agreement with you as well because, as a newbie, there's a lot of wording in there that may not resonate with you that you may not be aware of or you don't fully understand which could pop up later, wording that was in there to protect the seller and not you as the buyer.

Even with them trying to get out of a deal. In the purchase agreement that stated five days after doing due diligence, the contract is voided if he has not deposited the money. Now, you could be busy doing whatever, but you forgot to put that in there. That's dangerous because now you did all this due diligence, you'd have found the buyer, and now all of a sudden, they reneged out the deal because they breached the contract you had. You signed it and everything, both signed it, but you never sent the earnest money deposit. It could be stuff like that in there. Pay attention to the details, as the small things are the most important. Remember that.

Number three: Lease agreements

Lease agreements deal with tenants. You may have a property you purchased, and you rehab it for tenants. You do the bare minimum with materials, but it depends on the market. If you're doing rehab in a low-income area, I would highly recommend putting the B-grade materials in the properties, not the A-grade. A-grade materials are things like granite countertops and nice flooring. I'm talking about luxury style meant for a homeowner. I recommend that people go that route with A-grade material if you're putting tenants in them. But that's another story.

So lease agreements deal with tenants where you can sign an agreement on their terms: month to month, 12 months, 24 months, a two-year term. Now, I don't recommend anybody to do a two-year term. I recommend them to do a yearly tenant agreement because things change. You never know, and you don't want to be stuck with a tenant for two years if they're not paying or they're tearing up your house. Every year will give you a chance to reevaluate everything and see how they're treating your property. So in a lease agreement, I recommend that you put in there that the landlord or property management, however you word it, has the right, giving the tenant notice, to check up on the property on 24 hours notice. Or you may want to put in the lease agreement that you want to check on a property every 30 days or every quarter. Whatever you decide, what makes you feel comfortable, do it because this will protect your property. When they know that you're coming to check up on your property every month or every quarter, they're going to do their best to upkeep that property, making sure that there are no holes in the wall, etc. And another nugget I want to share with you is if you're doing lease agreements and you decide to go the leasing route and have tenants, make sure you don't get carpet. I got tired of replacing carpet every year, after every tenant. Go with hardwood floors, tile floors, or something hard that can be easily mopped up.

Number four: Transactional Close Agreement

Transactional Close Agreements deal with transactional fees. So I have a lender that does transactional loans for people who may not have the income, but they may have a deal that they had brought almost to the closing table but don't have the money to fund the deal. So these are guaranteed closings where they know you have the buyer, and you have the seller. With all the laws changing, some title companies don't accept the way I did it initially, where I didn't put any money down. I'd use someone else's money to buy the property. That's a no-no to some title companies. But I was lucky not to get stopped because it's different rules and laws in every state. Some states prohibit you from wholesaling because you must be a licensed realtor. I'm currently doing wholesale work in Detroit, Michigan, anywhere in Michigan. I know they've been trying to pass this law about making wholesalers become agents, but it's not going to happen. They've been saying that for years, they've been trying to get that closed down because I believe that they're getting mad, and agents are mad that they see us making money, hundreds of thousands of dollars, some of the millions through wholesaling. On the other hand, you have real estate agents who make 6%, or maybe they may have to split their commission with another agent that brought the deal to the table.

So transactional closings deal with deals that are already ready to close. And the title company may not honor you using somebody else's money to do the deal, to buy the property. So you have this person here, the middle person, the transactional guy or woman, put the money in escrow, and they may charge you $1,000 as a transactional fee. All the documents are submitted to the title company and put into a HUD statement which is then given to you. The HUD shows you all the expenses that will be taken out of your check.

Just know that all these documents are very important. And whenever you're doing the deal, putting all the pieces of the puzzle together is very important. These are all the pieces to the puzzle. You're going to need your agreement.

I told you earlier about my family's land story that we didn't have an operating agreement.

Oh, by the way, speaking of the operating agreement, that's another key document to have as well. The operating agreement will allow you to break everything down to who owns what and what percentage is owed to who. It also shows all the details of ownership percentages. It shows everything. So you know, when it comes to selling the company, if you ever had to sell the company with a joint venture partner, you can rightfully split up the funds or whatever money comes in, you can honor that contract. That's the right way of doing business. There's nothing shady about it. It's not that you don't trust the individual, but it is the right way to do business.

So, the word of caution. I'll tell you right now, do not do quitclaim deeds, only warranty deeds. I said this in one of my social media posts, don't skip over $1 to get a penny because you will lose every time. Always remember that. What do I mean by that? Well, I'm glad you asked. By not skipping over $1 to get a penny, I mean when you go the cheaper route trying to save money, you lose money and spend more money. I've made so many mistakes in the past where I went the cheaper route and ended up paying more money. Even with my early rehabs, I went with a skilled guy, but he wasn't licensed. Did you know that after spending about $40,000 in a house, a rehab, I had to go and another $40,000 to do it the right way with a licensed contractor? And I still didn't get it all the way completed because I ran out of capital. The property wasn't even worth more than $70,000 after repair value. So I was pretty much $80,000 in and had to sell it for a loss just to get my money back out of it. I'm talking about a moment of just frustration and sadness. But it's all good. That's why I'm here to tell you my failures so that you won't fail—you will succeed.

So always remember this: no quitclaim deeds, only warranty deeds. A quitclaim deed is an individual giving up all interests of that property and conveying it over to the new owner, to the person they quitclaim it to. And all that simply is is that person who quitclaims it to you, saying I have no responsibility for this property. I am conveying it over to this entity. I'm giving all interest, anything that involves me, I am giving it over to the buyer. This buyer is taking all the responsibilities for any blight tickets, any things that come up. That's all a quitclaim deed is. It's not giving you any warranty or anything. That person may not even have an interest in the property at all. The person may just know the actual owner. He may not even be on the title. He may not be on a deed. I know one thing for sure, it's easy to sue people, but it's harder to get that money back. I went through recent litigation with a guy that settled outside of court. He owed me $55,000 because he wasn't on the deed. He scammed me. He impersonated a legitimate company by adding an "s" at the end of his entity name to mirror the legit company. So when I did my title search on the property, I did my due diligence, everything checked out. This is how I learned about "doing the do." Now when I look at the articles, I can see who signed off on the papers and who's the registered agent. That's something I failed to do with this deal. I didn't see that individual's name in the articles. I'd seen his article, it was parallel, and it looked the same. To make a long story short, I couldn't go after the guy because it's harder to get your money back, but it's easy to sue. So I've been advised by my attorney to get what he can. We already gave him the demand letters. We served him papers, etc. But if I had known this, I would have never done it. But you live and learn, and that's what I'm doing. I'm teaching you from my mistakes. So do not buy a quitclaim deed. Get a warranty deed.

Even when you get a warranty deed, you want to make sure you close at a title company. You want to make sure you tell whoever's doing your title work, you want an owner's policy, you want a commitment. Where's my owner's policy commitment? You want a commitment. It shows that they're ensuring that this property that you're pursuing is free and clear of all taxes and liens and has nothing on there whatsoever; it's a clear title. You want to get a commitment from the title company so you can ensure that this title is clear and clean. It's called a title commitment. The title commitment will have all the details in there, and it will show how much is going to be backed up against, whether it's a $5 million owner's policy up to 5 million. And it's going to provide you with title companies licensing and everything.

So that's very important. Make sure you get a warranty deed with the owner's policy and get the title commitment from the title company because you could get a warranty deed that isn't warrantable. A person who is a novice, who does not understand real estate, who hasn't had that experience will think, oh, I have a warranty deed. No. It's a warranty deed but do you have insurance on it? Is there a homeowner's policy? Do you have that on there? If not, you're in trouble, and you might as well just get a quitclaim deed.

So that's the word of caution: no quitclaim deeds, only warranty deeds. And we know that you don't want to go the cheaper route because going the cheaper route will ultimately cost you more money.

CHAPTER 10

Building and Leveraging Your Personal Credit to Scale Your Business

My mentors told me that your credit is your life; credit is everything. For some of the wealthiest people I know, one of the ways they built their wealth was through their personal and business credit. There are ways that you can maximize the credit to get the things you need.

I utilized my credit for a business startup. It was a different business, different from real estate, but kind of tied to real estate where I got like a $50,000 line of credit. In Michigan, where I currently invest, there is a problem with squatters, so I used that line of credit to start a squatter removal service. This was my business credit, and I used it to buy more equipment and expand my company. There are all types of lending options out there for businesses. I recommend that people start with their personal credit because sometimes you have to be the grantor on that business credit that doesn't have any type of history. You may not even have a Dun & Bradstreet number or anything like that.

I've started something where I wanted to help individuals like the class and stuff I teach weekly. People complain, "I don't have money to start. I don't know how to start." So one of the ways I tell people to start is through their credit. And if they didn't have credit, I can repair their credit because all credit can be restored and rebuilt. You just have to follow the steps. I do offer that and all that's going to be provided at kerrylampkin.com. You can click one of those tabs on the website and explore what I have to offer regarding credit repair and business credit.

But I always recommend that we start with the personal credit because the personal credit is what they're going to go off sometimes if you have a startup company. I had to do that myself one day. So keep that in mind for personal credit.

So we talked about the importance of personal credit and how it can grow your business. The next thing, once you get your personal credit to a good score, you want to practice building your business credit. I have a done-for-you program that will help people build their business credit. It's going to teach you everything, including how to establish business credentials. How to establish your business name and how to choose a corporate entity. I'm also going to talk about requesting an EIN from the IRS. In this done-for-you program, I'm also going to talk about establishing business addresses. Because a lot of times whenever you have a business, they look at that, "Are you at an apartment building? Where are you?" You know that they look at that. They look at where your company is. That's why it's really good to have a virtual address. And I will teach more about personal credit in the DFY program.

There will be two different programs: a done-for-you program and a do-it-yourself program. So to do it yourself, I'm telling you the steps right now where things need to be done to understand the importance of building your business credit and how you can grow your business by doing this. Because I'm telling you, once you get this thing locked in, you'll be able to get from $150,000 to $250,000 to a million, all the way up to like $10 million in builder's funds. If you look at different corporations such as Walmart, Walmart has thousands and thousands in lines of credit from different banks. Look it up. You can Google it. Walmart has thousands and thousands of banks. I want to say they have like over 4,000 lines of credit from different banks. It's a large number of lines of credit that Walmart has. And that's not to mention other big corporations. So I'm teaching you how to do the same thing as these big corporations. This is what you have to do.

So back to establishing your business address, select the business address solution, then you're going to need to list the business with the 411 Directories. I'm going to select the business phone number for you because that's very important. I'm going to select a business fax number. That's also important as well. You want to establish yourself the right way. I said this before. You want to do things correctly. This is why many people and businesses are not succeeding and are not able to get the funding they need because they don't have these things in place. I'm also going to help you establish a business website. I have a web designer who will help you design your website the way your company functions and advise you on things you should do.

Keep in mind everything you need to get the business funding line of credit to maximize and leverage your business credit. You want to make sure you get trade lines. This is how you build your business credit and access different business funding options. So we're still talking about establishing business credit. Next, you're going to need to create your business email address. A lot of times, banks look at that too. They may see that your email is Kerryrlampkin@gmail. I'm supposed to be this big corporation, and my business email is Gmail—that's not professional. So you want to make sure you create a business email.

Next, you want to establish a business bank account. That is so important. How can you do business without a business account? You want to keep your personal and business accounts separate. They are separate entities. Treat your business like a human. Everything funded for a business needs to be in the business account. Everything funded as personal needs to be coming out of your personal account. So keep that in mind.

Next, I'm also going to ensure you have all the proper business licensing required in the place where you live. So, for example, we talked about the law in Michigan. We talked about how you can go to any Secretary of State online and form your articles, form your business. Before you decide on a business name, you can search to see if the name is available. That will save you a lot of time and from getting rejected by the Secretary of State. If somebody else has that name, you will get rejected.

I will have to verify your business listing with business credit agencies, which will help you get this business credit. And I know I'm going into great details about it, but the more details, the better. The more understanding you have, the better you can then know what you're getting into and get an understanding. So that's what I'm doing now. I'm giving you an understanding of how you can build your business credit to grow your business. This is big. We're talking about building and leveraging your credit and funding to scale your business.

So we've talked about establishing business credibility. Let's move on to talking about establishing business reports. This includes getting set up with a business credit reporting agency. Number one, setting up reporting with Dun & Bradstreet. I had to do that. I had to set up all my companies. I had to set up with Dun & Bradstreet because that's important. You have to do this yourself, too. When you pay things off, you can submit those payments to Dun & Bradstreet, which helps out a lot.

Number two, setting up reporting with Experian business. You have to report to these agencies. That's why setting up your business credit reporting with an agency is very important if you want to build rapport. If you want to show your company having business credit, this is very important. Setting up Equifax and NAV reports will be valuable steps for you to take.

Establish additional business credit. So that's another thing that I would do for you, or you could do it yourself, and I will give you pretty much a how-to and a guideline of what to do if you decide to do it yourself. So establishing additional business credit is like getting a credit card at Sam's Club or Costco. It's good to have business credit with those because the more credit you have on your business, the better. So when people pull your file, they look at, "Oh wow, he has this paid off, he has 14 accounts open," the better chances of you getting approved up to $150,000, and I will show you how to get that.

Next is the business financing program. So you build business credit via credit cards up to $150,000. Once you get these two steps done, I can help put you through the financing program to build business credit through credit cards. And once you get the credit cards, you have those credit cards on your account. It also makes your account stronger because when you're looking to get more funding from elsewhere, you're more likely to get approved. Keep in mind, as I said before, Walmart had thousands of lines of credit.

So in Credit Acceleration One, the done for you, I will talk about starting business credit. Round one is about establishing the first five trade lines. And in step two, I'm going to monitor the business reports. I'm going to help monitor all the business reports such as the NAV, the Dun & Bradstreet, the business Experian report, the Equifax reports, and so on.

Next, we will build your business credit and learn how to establish relationships with different credit cards. I will show you the strategic way that I do things to help you build your business credit. You must show some type of history on your credit by paying things on time. Sometimes I utilize my card to get different benefits, you know, different things I get back, money that I get back. There are a lot of benefits to these credit cards, and I will teach you how to take advantage later on in this program.

In round three, I'm going to build advanced business credit. I will help you apply for business credit cards and help you apply for lines of credit.

Then in step four, I'm going to build revolving accounts. So that's pretty much helping you apply for bank credit. Sometimes it's a little harder dealing with banks. Still, when you have this stuff set up the right way initially, as I told you with steps one and two of establishing your business credibility and establishing your business report, all this other stuff will come easy. You're able to then apply for these things and get them. This is about a six-month process, but it's worth it.

So if you want to learn more about building your own personal and business credit, I would highly recommend you go to Kerrylampkin.com and the credit section. There will be something that will give you directions on what to click on. It's either credit repair, or it will be business credit or personal credit.

I have affiliate links too. If you don't decide to take my program, I have affiliate links with different companies. I partnered with Novae Money with my guy Rico, who's been doing an awesome job in the Georgia area helping people build their personal credit and business credit. Also, he's just a good life coach in business. He's very good. So I highly recommend my guy Rico's company, Novae Money. That's the reason why I decided to partner with him because I've seen results, not only in others' lives but in my life as well. Novae helped me understand this business credit even more.

I also want to talk about how I can add you as an authorized user on one of my accounts or one of my business partner's accounts, where this will help build your business credit and your personal credit. All the good history that I have on my credit, you'll be added to that. So whenever you're trying to apply for something, when the underwriter looks at your credit, they see, "Oh, this guy has a good payment history. It looks good for you." The history, that's what they're looking at. These underwriters are looking at your payment history and how long that account's been open. That's very strong for your approval.

Knowledge Is Great, but Applied Knowledge Is Powerful and Where the Profits Are

S o what are your next steps? Well, your next steps should be to get started. One of the hardest things about getting started... *is getting started*. I find that to be so true. I used to have that mindset. I did not want to get started. I was nervous and thought I was going to fail. But check this out. I heard it from all the greats that sometimes have to fail your way to success.

It's a learning process. What happens when you go to school? When you go to school, you learn, right? Even when you go off to college, you have to pay for that curriculum. You have to pay for those courses. You have to pay for that knowledge. It's the same because when you make a mistake, you learn from that mistake. I know it may be a little hard to think of it in that type of way, but that's how I see it. The mistakes you make are really to help you become better and become stronger. Your next step should be getting started to make it happen.

There's no such thing as getting this information that I provided you with, and you don't act on it. So action is everything. Action is everything. Don't be that person that reads and says, "Well, one day…" woulda, coulda, shoulda. You don't want to give one of those speeches to your children or anyone else. Just know that when you get knowledge, you need to apply that knowledge because that's the most powerful thing, actually applying it. Believe it or not, other people are watching you, looking up to you. And you don't want to be their failure. So you have to see it in that type of light. There's always someone watching you. There's always someone learning from you. And we're meant to help others and make an impact. Reach one, teach one.

So when you go to my website, just go to the link. You can book a 15-minute call with me to discuss all the details about this, everything we spoke about, and how you can get started. If you need help, I can be your coach. I will coach you through. We could talk about real estate, my real estate journey. We could talk about how to plan. We could talk about funding options. Whatever it is, we can map it out. We can map out a plan, and I can get you there. There's no failure on my team. It's all about winning—we all win.

And I want to say this. Nothing escapes the law of process. Everything always has different steps in order the way it should be done. When you skip the process, that's when things don't happen the right way. So everything I've told you about real estate and the secrets that I've obtained through my experience, I'm telling you to follow my steps, and you will succeed. Even when I told you not to make my mistakes, I was actually teaching you what not to do. So always remember this, nothing escapes the law of process. So get started!

THANK YOU FOR READING MY BOOK!

DOWNLOAD YOUR FREE GIFTS

Just to say thanks for buying and reading my book, I would like to give you a few free bonus gifts, no strings attached!

To Download Now, Visit:
www.WhyRealEstateBook.com/KLFreegifts

I appreciate your interest in my book, and I value your feedback as it helps me improve future versions of this book. I would appreciate it if you could leave your invaluable review on Amazon.com with your feedback. Thank you!